Looking at

Animals in
HOT
PLACES

Published by Raintree Steck-Vaughn Publishers,
an imprint of Steck-Vaughn Company

Series Editor Honor Head
Series Designer Hayley Cove
Picture Researcher Juliet Duff
Map Artwork Robin Carter / Wildlife Art Agency
Animal Symbols Arlene Adams

Raintree Steck-Vaughn Publishers Staff
Project Manager: Joyce Spicer
Editor: Pam Wells
Cover Design: Gino Coverty

Library of Congress Cataloging-in-Publication Data
Butterfield, Moira, 1961–
Animals in hot places / Moira Butterfield.
p. cm. — (Looking at)
Includes index.
Summary: Presents various animals that live in such hot places as deserts, rain forests, and grasslands, and describes how they adapt to their environment.
ISBN 0-7398-0112-0 (Hardcover) ISBN 0-7398-0715-3 (Softcover)
1. Desert animals — Juvenile literature. 2. Rain forest animals —
Juvenile literature. 3. Grassland animals — Juvenile literature.
[1. Desert animals. 2. Rain forest animals. 3. Grassland animals.]
I. Title. II. Series: Butterfield, Moira, 1961– Looking at —
QL 116.B78 1999
591.754 — dc21   99-10180
CIP

Printed in China
1 2 3 4 5 6 7 8 9 0 LB 02 01 00 99

Photographic credits
Frank Lane Picture Agency: 7, 27, 28 E. & D. Hosking; 10 Panda/S. Vannini;
13, 22, and 26 Gerard Lacz; 16 Leeson/Sunset; 18 Ron Austing;
19 Lewis W. Walker; 20 Chris Mattison; 29 Leonard Lee Rue. NHPA:
21 Stephen Dalton. Planet Earth Pictures: 12 Alain Dragesco;
17 Richard Coomber. Oxford Scientific Films: 6 Mickey Gibson;
8, 15 Michael Fogden; 9 London Scientific Films; 11 Konrad White;
14 Kathie Atkinson; 23 Root/Okapia; 24 Mike Linley; 25 J.A.L. Cooke.
Cover credit Scorpion: Oxford Scientific Films/Michael Fogden

Looking at

Animals in

HOT PLACES

Moira Butterfield

RSVP

RAINTREE
STECK-VAUGHN
P U B L I S H E R S
A Steck-Vaughn Company

Austin, Texas

www.steck-vaughn.com

Introduction

There are many parts of the world where it is very hot. These hot places are deserts, rain forests, and grasslands.

Some deserts have hardly any rain, and here there is nothing but sand. Other deserts are made of rocks and boulders.

In some deserts it rains very hard once a year. Rain forests have a lot of rain and are very hot and steamy all year long. Grasslands are very dry most of the time, but they have lots of rain once a year.

Many animals live in these hot places, from tiny insects and strange looking lizards, to birds and big animals. They all have their own ways of living in the heat.

Contents

Camel

Camels live in deserts that are hot and dry. They can go without food and water for many days. Their feet are big and wide, which helps them to walk on soft sand. In the deserts of Africa, people often use camels instead of cars to carry them around.

Scorpion

Scorpions live in hot places, but they hide in the shade during the day. They come out at night when it is cooler.

Scorpions eat insects and spiders. They kill them with their strong claws. Scorpions sting and kill big insects with the stinger on the end of their tail.

Gorilla

Gorillas live in jungles that are hot and steamy. They eat lots of fruits, vines, and leaves. They live in big family groups, headed by the strongest male. Adult gorillas can be three times as big as a grown man. Gorillas climb trees where they build a nest to sleep in.

Sand Cat

The little sand cat lives in northern Africa. It is wild, not tame and friendly like a pet cat. It prowls around at night looking for mice and snakes to eat.

It has sharp teeth and claws. The bottom of its paws are hairy, so it can walk on hot sand and not burn its paws.

Moloch Lizard

Lizards like hot places. This prickly moloch lizard lives in a desert in Australia. Sometimes it is called a thorny devil because its back is covered with sharp spines. The spines keep other animals from attacking it. It has a long tongue that it uses to lick up ants from the ground.

Tapir

Tapirs live in swamps or near streams in the jungle. They sleep in the daytime and come out at night when it is cool. They eat water plants and leaves.

The tapir swims well. This means it can escape bigger animals, such as jaguars, who would like to eat tapirs.

Elf Owl

Birds live in hot places, too. This tiny elf owl is about the size of a coffee mug. It lives in the Southwest. The owl is too small to make its own hole, so it looks for one that a bigger bird has made. It lays its eggs in a hole in a tall, prickly cactus. There they will be safe from harm.

Rattlesnake

Snakes love warmth, so hot places are good homes for them. This rattlesnake lives on deserts in the United States. It has sharp, poisonous fangs.

This snake has tiny scales at the end of its tail. When it rattles them, it sends a message that means, "Stay away!"

Hippopotamus

Hippos live in Africa. They spend the day keeping cool in the lakes and rivers. They leave the water at night to eat grasses and plants. Though they are very big and heavy, they are good swimmers. Hippos are very fierce and have huge teeth. They often fight each other.

Spadefoot Toad

One kind of American spadefoot toad has big feet for digging burrows in the desert. This toad hides underground for most of the year waiting for rain to come.

When the rain comes, the toad hops out to lay its eggs in the puddles. The babies grow into adults in just two weeks.

Fennec

The fennec is a kind of fox that lives in African deserts. It digs its burrow in the sand and lives in it. It has big ears that help it hear well and keep cool. When the little fox gets too hot, the heat from inside its body passes out through its ears, just like heat coming out of a radiator.

Tarantula

The red-kneed tarantula spider lives in deserts in Mexico. It hides in a burrow underground. It puts a few tiny silk threads outside the opening of its burrow.

When a small animal walks by, the threads wobble. Then, the tarantula jumps out and bites it with its poisonous fangs.

Where They Live

This map of the world shows you where the animals live.

NORTH
AMERICA

SOUTH
AMERICA

desert

rain forest

grassland

 camel

 scorpion

 gorilla

 sand cat

 moloch lizard

 tapir

 elf owl

 rattlesnake

 hippopotamus

 spadefoot toad

 fennec

 tarantula

EUROPE

ASIA

AFRICA

AUSTRALIA

Index of Words to Learn